THE BASEBALL KITCHEN

Recipes to Go with Your Favorite Baseball Team

DAVID & MADALON WILSON

Balboa Press books may be ordered through booksellers or by contacting:

Balboa Press
A Division of Hay House
1663 Liberty Drive
Bloomington, IN 47403
www.balboapress.com
1-(877) 407-4847

Because of the dynamic nature of the Internet, any web addresses or links contained in this book may have changed since publication and may no longer be valid. The views expressed in this work are solely those of the author and do not necessarily reflect the views of the publisher, and the publisher hereby disclaims any responsibility for them.

Certain stock imagery © Thinkstock.
Any people depicted in stock imagery provided by Thinkstock are models,
and such images are being used for illustrative purposes only.

ISBN: 978-1-4525-5779-3 (e)
ISBN: 978-1-4525-5778-6 (sc)

Printed in the United States of America

Balboa Press rev. date: 9/4/2012

The story behind *The Baseball Kitchen Cookbook* began years ago when David & Madalon first started their family. David used the yearly winners of the World Series to remember important dates.

We were married during a year when the Reds won so the important date was commemorated by the Cincinnati Reds World Series win. Dave was born in 1952, so he became a Yankee baby and Madalon, born in 1954 was a Giant baby. When our oldest daughter, Jennifer was born in 1977, the Yankees won the series. She became a Yankee baby. Then in 1979 when Angela was born she was a Pirate baby. Our youngest daughter Amberly, born in 1984, became a Tiger baby. This evolved into a fun way to assign duties and since we lived on a farm, feeding the animals in addition to household chores. We would watch the standings daily and the losing teams, whether it was the Yankees, Pirates, Tigers or Giants would be on specific duties that day.

As time passed, we taught the girls to cook. Dave, being the more creative cook in the family, passed on his creative imagination and Madalon passed on the importance of measuring and writing down the new recipe. We have also taken yearly baseball trips to see a major league game and enjoy the whole baseball experience.

The next natural step, since the girls were getting older and starting their own families, was to combine baseball teams with cooking. We began researching the locations of the teams and finding foods that were popular and fit in with the local culture. Now when we watched the All Star Game and the World Series and other games, we would put together a menu that would go with the city the game was taking place in.

Baseball Kitchen is more than a cookbook. It is a visual story of family togetherness and unity. Now in addition to cooking and watching baseball with our children, it has become a way to enjoy cooking and baseball with our grandchildren. We hope you enjoy our family's journey through baseball.

David and Madalon Wilson

P.S. Yes, our grandchildren have their own team from the year they were born. Here they are:

    Alanys- Yankee baby
    Chance- Marlin baby
    Alexie- Yankee baby
    Haylie- Marlin baby
    Isabel- Philly baby

Enchilada Pie

12-16 corn tortillas

4 grilled and chopped chicken breasts

2-10 ounce cans enchilada sauce

1-15 ounce chili with beans

Frito corn chips

1-10 ounce can chopped olives

Shredded cheddar cheese

Butter flavored cooking spray

2 chopped onions

2 chopped green chiles

1. Grill and cut up chicken breasts and set aside.
2. Saute onion and chiles and set aside.
3. Spray a glass cake pan with cooking spray.(9x12)
4. Layer the pan with 6-8 tortillas.
5. Generously add a layer of onions, olives and chiles.
6. Pour 1 can of enchilada sauce on evenly.
7. Sprinkle on a generous layer of cheese.
8. Spread on a layer of chili beans.
9. Add a layer of corn chips.
10. Spread all the chicken on the next layer.
11. Layer 6-8 tortillas on the top.
12. Pour the other can of enchilada sauce over the top.
13. Add another generous helping of cheese over the sauce.
14. Bake in the oven at 400 degrees for 15-20 minutes.
15. Enjoy during the Diamondbacks game.

Enchilada Pie

Southwest Pancakes

2 cups flour	2 eggs
1 cup corn meal	2 cups buttermilk
1 tablespoon baking powder	¼ cup vegetable or canola oil
1 teaspoon baking soda	Butter
1 cup sour cream	Prickly pear syrup

1. Mix all the dry ingredients in a bowl.
2. Stir in the eggs, buttermilk, sour cream, and oil.
3. For thinner pancakes add a little more buttermilk.
4. For thicker pancakes add a little more flour.
5. Melt a little butter on a griddle on medium heat.
6. Pour some of the pancake mix over the butter on the hot griddle.
7. With a spatula, flip the pancake over when tiny bubbles appear.
8. Serve with butter and prickly pear syrup.
9. Enjoy during the Diamondbacks game.

Southwest Pancakes

Southern Fried Chicken

1 chicken, cut up for frying

4 eggs

1 cup hot sauce

½ cup milk

2 cups bisquick

½ cup parmesan cheese

1 teaspoon salt

1 teaspoon ground black pepper

1 teaspoon paprika

1 teaspoon garlic powder

Peanut oil

1. Have 2 separate bowls.
2. In 1 bowl beat the eggs and add the hot sauce and milk.
3. In the other bowl mix all the dry ingredients.
4. Dip each piece of chicken in the egg mix.
5. Then coat each piece of chicken with the dry mixture.
6. Fry in medium hot peanut oil for 6-8 minutes per side.
7. Enjoy during the Braves game.

Southern Fried Chicken

Peach Cobbler

1-18 ounce package
yellow or vanilla cake mix
(most mixes require
3 eggs,1/3 cup vegetable oil,
1 ¼ cup water)

6-8 peaches

1 cup sugar

1 teaspoon cinammon

½ cups of Minute tapioca

Whipped Cream

1. Peel and slice peaches
2. Stir in sugar, cinammon, and tapioca with the peaches and set aside.
3. Mix cake batter as directed.
4. Put peach mixture in a 13x9 pan.
5. Pour cake batter over the peaches.
6. Bake at 350 degrees for 35-40 minutes.
7. Cool for 20 minutes, then serve with whipped cream.
8. Enjoy during the Braves game.

Peach Cobbler

Crab Cakes

12-14 ounces crab meat

1 1/3 cup Panko bread crumbs

1 teaspoon basil

1 egg

5-6 tablespoons mayonnaise

2 Tablespoons Worcestershire sauce

4 teaspoons Dijon mustard

Pinch salt and pepper

4 tablespoons vegetable oil

2 tablespoons butter

1 lemon

1 cup Greek yogurt

1 teaspoon dill

1 cucumber

1. Mix crab meat, crumbs, mayonnaise, Worcestershire sauce, mustard, salt and pepper in a bowl.
2. Stir in beaten egg.
3. Add more crumbs if desired.
4. Form 8-12 patties.
5. Cook patties in hot oil and butter mix.
6. Lightly brown on both sides.

For Greek yogurt sauce

1. Mix dill, lemon zest, and cucumber in a separate bowl.
2. Pour over crab cakes and squeeze lemon as desired on each crab cake.
3. Eat during the Orioles game.

Crab Cakes

Oyster Stew

1 cup chopped celery

1 cup chopped onion

1 quart half and half

2- 8 ounce cans whole oysters

Salt

Pepper

Celery salt

Cayenne pepper

3 tablespoons flour

2 tablespoons Worcestershire sauce

6 pieces chopped bacon

1. Fry chopped up bacon.
2. Saute onions and celery with the bacon, set aside.
3. In a large soup pan pour in the half and half.
4. Whisk in the flour.
5. Heat, but don't boil.
6. Add in the oysters and heat for a few more minutes.
7. Add in the bacon, onions, celery, and Worcestershire sauce.
8. Add in salt, pepper, celery salt, and cayenne pepper to taste.
9. Enjoy during the Oriole game.

Oyster Stew

Broiled Lobster Tails

2 whole lobster tails
1 cube butter, melted
½ teaspoon paprika

Salt to taste
Ground white pepper to taste
1 lemon

1. Cut top of lobster tails lengthwise.
2. Pull apart shells part way.
3. Season meat with butter, salt, paprika, and pepper.
4. Broil for 5 or 10 minutes or until meat is opaque.
5. Use lemon juice as desired.
6. Dip meat in melted butter.
7. Enjoy during the Red Sox game.

Broiled Lobster Tails

Boston Baked Beans

2-15 ounce cans navy beans

½ pound bacon

1 diced onion

¼ cup sorghum or molasses

2 teaspoons salt

½ teaspoon pepper

¼ teaspoon dry mustard

½ cup ketchup

¼ cup brown sugar

3 or 4 dashes of Worcestershire sauce

1. Fry the bacon
2. Saute' onions with bacon set aside after 5 minutes.
3. Pour beans in casserole dish.
4. Cover with bacon and onions.
5. Pour on bacon grease (optional)
6. Mix the rest of the ingredients in a pan and bring to a boil.
7. Pour over the beans.
8. Cover with lid or foil.
9. Cook in the oven for 30 minutes at 325 degrees.
10. Eat during the Red Sox game

Boston Baked Beans

Chicago Dogs

All beef franks	Tomato wedges
Poppy seed buns	Dill pickle spears
Yellow mustard	Sport peppers
Neon green relish	Celery salt
Chopped white onions	

1. Place the franks in very hot water for about 20-25 minutes (not boiling).
2. Steam the poppy seed buns.
3. Place a frank on the steamed bun.

To be authentic, add the condiments in this order:

4. Spread the mustard on the beef frank.
5. Now spread on the relish.
6. Sprinkle on the chopped onions.
7. Put 2 tomato wedges on each hot dog.
8. Add one pickle spear.
9. Now add 2 sport peppers.
10. Sprinkle with celery salt.
11. Enjoy during the Cubs game.

Chicago Dogs

Summer Sausages

Lots of little smoked summer sausages

3 or 4 bottles of your favorite barbeque sauce

¼ cup grape jelly

Crockpot

1. Fill the crockpot ¾ full of sausages.
2. Mix the barbeque sauce and the grape jelly together.
3. Add to the crockpot.
4. Stir in well with the sausages.
5. Cover and heat on low for 2 hours.
6. Enjoy during the Cubs game.

Summer Sausages

Chicago Deep Dish Pizza

2 packages frozen pizza dough

4 pounds Italian sausage

40 slices pepperoni

1 large diced onion

1 large diced bell pepper

1 package cut up mushrooms

4 - 7 ounce cans crushed tomatoes

3 pounds shredded mozzerella cheese

4 tablespoons grated parmesan cheese

3 tablespoons Italian seasoning

Cooking spray

Flour

1. Let the pizza dough thaw out overnight in the refrigerator.
2. Roll out the dough with a little flour to prevent sticking.
3. In a deep pan or glass dish, spread the rolled dough evenly, coming up the sides.
4. In a frying pan, brown the sausage. Set aside.
5. Saute the onions, peppers, and mushrooms for just a few minutes.
6. Add the vegetables to the sausage.
7. Put the shredded cheese on top of the dough in the pan.
8. Add the sausage and vegetable mixture.
9. Cover with the crushed tomatoes.
10. Put the pepperoni on top.
11. Sprinkle the parmesan cheese and Italian seasoning over the top.
12. Bake in a 450 degree oven for 20 minutes or until the crust is a golden brown.
13. Enjoy during the White Sox game.

Chicago Deep Dish Pizza

Soft Pretzels

5 cups flour

1 tablespoon sugar

1 ½ teaspoons salt

1 package active dry yeast

1 ½ cups warm water (110 degrees)

¾ cup baking soda

5 cups boiling water

Coarse or kosher salt to taste

Vegetable oil

1 beaten egg

1. Mix the sugar, salt, yeast and warm water together.
2. In a food processor add in the flour a little at a time. Mix until dough is smooth. You may not need the entire 5 cups of flour.
3. Let the dough rise from 45 minutes to an hour.
4. Take several chunks of the dough and roll each one into a long piece.
5. Shape it into a pretzel.
6. Boil 5 cups of water with baking soda.
7. Place each pretzel in the boiling water, one at a time. Do this for about 20 seconds.
8. Coat a pan or cookie sheet with vegetable oil and with a spatula put the pretzels in the pan.
9. Salt each pretzel with course or kosher salt.
10. Brush each pretzel with the egg. Cook in the oven at 450 degrees for 12- 15 minutes or until golden brown.
11. Enjoy during the White Sox game.

Soft Pretzels

Molasses Roasted Pork

3-4 pounds pork roast

1 cup molasses

1 cup brown sugar

3 chopped or sliced carrots

3 stalks chopped celery

1 small chopped onion

½ cup apple cider vinegar

¼ cup dijon mustard

½ teaspoon celery salt

½ teaspoon red pepper

1 teaspoon sage

¼ teaspoon thyme

Salt and pepper to taste

Molasses Roasted Pork

1. Mix molasses, brown sugar, vinegar, mustard, celery salt, red pepper, sage and thyme in a bowl. Add salt and pepper as desired.

2. Baste mixture on the pork roast in a cooking pan.

3. Refrigerate for 2 or 3 hours or overnight.

4. Take out of the refrigerator and spoon molasses mixture over the roast.

5. Spread the carrots, celery, and onion over the top of the roast.

6. Bake in a 450 degree oven for 90 minutes or more.

7. Make sure a thermometer reads 160 degrees when put in the center of the meat.

8. Serve during the Reds game.

Cincinnati Chili

1 chopped onion

1 ½ pounds ground beef

2 cloves minced garlic

1 teaspoon cumin

1 teaspoon cinnamon

1 teaspoon allspice

2 tablespoons chili powder

Dash of salt

2 tablespoons of unsweetened cocoa

2 tablespoons Worcestershire sauce

2 tablespoons apple cider vinegar

1-15 ounce can tomato sauce

¼ cup water

¼ cup vegetable oil

1 small package of spaghetti pasta

the following toppings if desired

More chopped onion

Oyster Crackers

Small can of kidney beans

Shredded cheddar cheese

Cincinnati Chili

1. Cook the ground beef in a large frying pan and set aside.

2. Saute' the onion and garlic in vegetable oil.

3. Add cummin, cinnamon, allspice, chili powder, Worcestershire sauce, vinegar to the onions and garlic.

4. Add the above to the ground beef and mix in.

5. Stir in the tomato sauce and simmer for 45 minutes.

6. While the ground beef mixture is simmering cook the spaghetti according to the directions on the package.

7. When spaghetti is done, place on plates for individual servings.

8. Now spoon the chili mixture on top of the spaghetti on each plate.

9. Use toppings as desired from the onions, Oyster crackers, kidney beans, and cheese.

10. 2 way is chili on the pasta, 3 way is also with cheese, 4 way is also with onions, and 5 way has kidney beans and everything else.

11. Serve during the Reds game. I like mine 5 way with lots of cheese.

Polish Boy

Polish sausages

Hot dog or hoagie buns

Potatoes cut up for fries

Vegetable oil

Bar-b-q sauce

½ head cabbage

1 carrot

¼ cup vinegar

2 teaspoons sugar

¼ cup mayonnaise

2 Tablespoons bacon bits

1. To make coleslaw, use a food processor.
2. Shred the cabbage and carrot in a food processor.
3. Put shredded mix in a bowl and add vinegar, sugar, mayonnaise, and bacon bits.
4. Stir together for coleslaw.
5. Using vegetable oil, on high heat, in a deep fryer or frying pan, fry the potatoes into french fries.
6. Toast the buns in a toaster oven.
7. Cook the Polish sausages in the hot vegetable oil until almost black.
8. Place cooked sausage on a toasted bun.
9. As desired, add fries, coleslaw, and your favorite bar-b-q sauce as toppings.
10. Enjoy during the Indians game.

Polish Boy

Chicken Pot Pie

1 large onion

½ pound mushrooms

1 cup celery

3 cups frozen peas and carrots

1 ½ pounds skinless chicken breasts

1 tub Philly Cream Cheese

2 cans chicken broth

½ cube butter

1/3 cup flour

1 tablespoon corn starch

2 deep dish pie crusts

Chicken Pot Pie

1. Melt butter in large saucepan
2. Add onions, mushrooms, and celery.
3. Saute' for a few minutes.
4. Add broth, peas and carrots, flour, and corn starch.
5. Let simmer while cooking the chicken.
6. Cube the chicken and cook in frying pan.
7. Add cooked chicken to the rest of the ingredients.
8. Pour mixture into pie crust and put other pie crust on top.
9. Bake at 400 degrees for 25 minutes.
10. Eat during the Indians game.

Rainbow Trout

1-4 trout

¼ cup flour

¼ cup corn meal

¼ cup milk

3 Tablespoons parmesan cheese

1 teaspoon paprika

1 lemon

½ teaspoon salt

½ teaspoon black pepper

1 stick butter

½ cup olive oil

½ cup slivered almonds

Dressing

½ cup mayonnaise

¼ cup sour cream

¼ cup chopped onion

¼ cup chopped cucumber

½ lemon

1. Mix flour, corn meal, parmesan cheese, paprika, salt, and pepper in a dish.
2. Pour the milk into a pan. Dip the trout in the milk and coat the wet trout in the flour mixture.
3. Heat the oil and ½ stick butter so it is hot.
4. Place the trout in the hot oil and butter and cook on high heat for 1 minute.
5. Turn the trout and cook for 1 more minute.
6. Reduce heat and cook each side for 5-6 minutes.
7. Mix the mayonnaise and sour cream for the dressing.
8. Add in the onions, and cucumbers, squeeze lemon juice into the mixture.
9. Serve on the side with the trout.
10. Melt ½ stick butter with the almonds.
11. Pour butter and almond mix on the trout, then garnish with lemon juice.
12. Enjoy during the Rockies game.

Rainbow Trout

Denver Omelet

2 beaten eggs

1/3 cup sliced mushrooms

¼ cup chopped onion

¼ cup green and red bell peppers

¼ cup chopped ham

½ cup shredded cheddar cheese

Salt

Black pepper

Butter

1. In a pan, saute the mushrooms, onions, peppers and ham, then set aside.
2. On medium heat, melt some butter in a frying pan.
3. Pour in the eggs.
4. Put all the mushrooms, onions, peppers, and ham on top of the eggs.
5. Put a lid on the pan and let cook for a few minutes.
6. Now gently slide a spatula under half of the omelette and fold it over the other half.
7. Put the lid back on the pan and cook for 1-2 more minutes.
8. When the omelette is done slide the spatula under it and transfer to a plate.
9. Sprinkle cheese over the top.
10. Serve with hash browns if desired.
11. Enjoy during the Rockies game.

Denver Omelet

Coney Island Dogs

8 all beef franks

1 pound ground beef

8 hot dog buns

1-8 ounce can tomato paste

2 minced garlic cloves

2 tablespoons brown sugar

3 tablespoons chili powder

1 tablespoon Worestershire sauce

1 teaspoon celery seed

1 teaspoon cumin

½ teaspoon ground pepper

2 tablespoons cider vinegar

1 tablespoon hot sauce

1 cup grated cheddar cheese

1 diced yellow onion

Mustard

1. Brown the ground beef in a frying pan.
2. Stir in ¾ of the diced onions and cook until translucent.
3. Stir in tomato paste.
4. Add in the garlic, brown sugar, chilli powder, Worcestershire sauce, celery seed, cumin, pepper, vinegar, and hot sauce.
5. Stir and mix well over low heat.
6. Add the franks to the mix.
7. Cover and simmer for about 20 minutes.
8. Steam the buns or microwave for 30 seconds.
9. Put ground beef, tomato mixture on the bun, and place a frank on top.
10. Sprinkle on a few diced onions.
11. Add mustard and grated cheese.
12. Enjoy during the Tigers game.

Coney Island Dogs

Tiger Stripe Rice Cereal Treats

6 cups chocolate rice crisp cereal

6 cups rice crisp cereal

2-10 ounce packages miniature marshmallows

1 stick butter

2 drops red food coloring

10 drops yellow food coloring

Cooking Spray

1. In a large cooking pan melt half a stick of butter.
2. Add 1 package of marshmallows.
3. Stir until melted.
4. Remove from heat and mix in chocolate rice cereal.
5. Mold 2 or 3 lengths in a 13x9 pan coated with cooking spray, several inches apart from one another.
6. In another large cooking pan melt a half stick of butter.
7. Add I package of marshmallows.
8. Add in the red and yellow food coloring.
9. Stir until melted.
10. Remove from heat and mix in rice cereal.
11. Mold 2 or 3 lengths and put between the chocolate cereal so it resembles tiger stripes.
12. Let cool for 10-15 minutes.
13. Eat during the Tigers game.

Tiger Stripe Rice Cereal Treats

Shrimp Fajitas

6 flour or corn tortillas

30-40 cleaned shrimp, no tails

1 package fajita seasoning

1 green bell pepper

1 red bell pepper

2-3 chili peppers

1 medium-large onion

Vegetable oil

Aluminum foil

Sour cream

Guacamole

Spanish rice

Refried beans

Lime

1. Slice all the peppers in thin strips.
2. Dice the onion.
3. Saute the peppers and onions in a frying pan with hot vegetable oil. Sprinkle with fajita seasoning.
4. Set aside.
5. Put the tortillas in foil and heat in the oven for 15 minutes at 350 degrees.
6. Saute' the shrimp until done in the vegetable oil. Sprinkle with fajita seasoning.
7. Remove tortillas from the oven
8. Place shrimp, onions, and peppers in the tortillas. Squeeze on lime juice
9. Garnish with sour cream and guacamole if desired
10. Serve with rice and beans.

Shrimp Fajitas

Dixie Salad

5 apples
4 pomegranites
8 ounces chopped walnuts

12 ounces whipped cream
(or whipped topping)
1 lemon
½ teaspoon cinnamon

1. Core and slice apples with apple slicer.
2. Chop apple slices in ½ inch pieces.
3. Take seeds out of pomegranites.
4. Chop walnuts.
5. Mix in a large bowl.
6. Add cinnamon.
7. Squeeze lemon juice over the mixture.
8. Fold in whipped cream.
9. Enjoy during the Astros game.

Dixie Salad

KC BBQ Sandwich

1-5 pound beef brisket

4 tablespoons liquid smoke

1 teaspoon salt

1 teaspoon ground black pepper

1 teaspoon celery salt

1 teaspoon garlic powder

1 teaspoon paprika

4 tablespoons Worcestershire sauce

1 teaspoon sage

1 bottle KC BBQ sauce

White bread or hamburger buns.

1. Several hours before cooking, put the liquid smoke and Worcestershire sauce on the brisket.
2. Rub in the seasonings.
3. Cover and refrigerate for 5 or more hours.
4. In a cooking pan, cover the brisket with foil and cook for about 5 hours at 280 degrees.
5. Take it out of the oven and scrape off the fat.
6. Pour a cup of BBQ sauce over the brisket.
7. Place uncovered in the oven for 20 more minutes.
8. Take out of the oven and let cool for a half hour.
9. Now slice the brisket into ¼ inch slices and put it on white bread or a hamburger bun.
10. Enjoy during the Royals game.

KC BBQ Sandwich

Ozark Pudding

2 eggs

¾ cup white sugar

1 cup brown sugar

½ cup flour

3 teaspoons baking powder

¾ teaspoon salt

1 tablespoon vanilla extract

2 cups chopped apples

1 ½ cups chopped walnuts

Cream/whipped cream/ice cream

1. Beat the eggs and the sugar.
2. Add in the flour, baking powder,salt, and vanilla.
3. Mix well.
4. Fold in the apples and walnuts.
5. Bake in a small greased cake pan.
6. Bake at 350 degrees for 40 minutes or until done.
7. Serve during the Royals game with your choice of cream, whipped cream, or ice cream.
   I like mine with fresh cream.

Ozark Pudding

Chili Rellenos

6 Anaheim long green chilis

1 cup flour

1 cup cornmeal

6 eggs

1 tablespoon oregano

2 tablespoons cilantro seasoning

3 minced garlic cloves

6 thick rectangular slices Monterey Jack cheese

Mild or hot salsa

Vegetable oil

½ teaspoon salt

½ teaspoon ground black pepper

1. Slice each pepper and remove seeds.
2. Slice one side so the pepper can be stuffed.
3. In hot oil cook the peppers on both sides for 1-2 minutes.
4. Set peppers aside for a few minutes, then peel the outer skin from each pepper.
5. Put the flour in one bowl and the corn meal in another.
6. With the eggs, separate the white from the yolk.
7. Beat the white until it is fluffy.
8. Fold in the yolks.
9. Add oregano, cilantro, garlic, salt and black pepper to the eggs.
10. Take each Anaheim chili and roll them in the flour.
11. Dip peppers in the egg mixture. Coat the inside and outside well.
12. Roll peppers in the cornmeal.
13. Put a generous amount of cheese inside each chili.
14. Place the chilis on a large cookie pan.
15. Bake in the oven for 15 minutes at 400 degrees.
16. Remove from oven and put salsa on each chili.
17. Enjoy during the Angels game.

Chili Rellenos

Angel Cake

12 egg whites

1 ¼ cup powdered sugar

1 cup sugar blended

1 cup sifted white flour

1 teaspoon vanilla extract

¼ teaspoon salt

Sliced strawberries

Strawberry glaze

Whipped Cream

1. Sift the flour, stir in the sugars and set aside.
2. With an electric mixer beat the egg whites until you have firm peaks.
3. Gently fold in the flour and sugar with the beaten egg whites.
4. Add the salt and vanilla.
5. Pour the batter into an angel cake pan. Do not grease the pan.
6. Cook in the oven for 30-35 minutes at 350 degrees.
7. When finished, invert the pan, gently slip a knife around the sides to release the cake.
8. After cooling for 10 or 15 minutes spread the cake with the strawberry glaze.
9. Add a liberal amount of strawberries.
10. Top with whipped cream.
11. Enjoy during the Angel game.

Angel Cake

Burrito

2 pounds ground beef, shredded pork, beef, or chicken

Several large flour tortillas

1 package taco seasoning

1-8 ounce package cream cheese

1 onion, diced

2-3 jalapeno peppers, diced

1-14 ounce can diced tomatoes

1 package enchilada seasoning

Shredded lettuce

Shredded cheddar cheese

1. In a large frying pan brown the meat.
2. Add cream cheese and taco seasoning to the meat and let simmer with a lid on.
3. In another pan saute' the onions and peppers.
4. Stir in the onions and peppers with the meat.
5. In a sauce pan, warm the tomatoes with the enchilada seasoning.
6. Spoon the meat mixture in each tortilla.
7. Fold tortilla and spoon tomato mixture over the top.
8. Sprinkle a liberal amount of cheese on top.
9. Warm in the microwave 30-60 seconds.
10. Top with lettuce.
11. Enjoy during the Dodgers game.

Burrito

Corn Dodgers

3 eggs

½ cup milk

1 cup corn flakes

1 cup corn meal

½ cup grated parmesan cheese

1 cup cheddar cheese crackers

1 cup soda crackers

1 small diced onion

1 can corn

½ teaspoon ground black pepper

½ teaspoon oregano

Vegetable oil

1. In a separate bowl blend the eggs and milk together.
2. In a food processor, blend all the dry ingredients together.
3. Mix the blended crumbs with the egg and milk.
4. Add the onions and corn.
5. If batter is too moist, add more corn meal or crackers.
6. If the batter is too dry add a little milk.
7. Roll into balls.
8. Fry on medium high heat in vegetable oil.
9. When golden brown turn over and finish cooking.
10. Serve during the Dodger game.

Corn Dodgers

Grilled Swordfish

4 or 5 swordfish or marlin steaks

¼ cup apple cider vinegar

¼ cup soy sauce

¼ cup olive oil

1 tablespoon chicken tarragon seasoning

1 teaspoon ground sage

½ teaspoon lemon pepper seasoning

1 lemon

Cucumber Sauce

1 diced cucumber

1 small diced stalk celery

½ small, diced onion

1 – 16 oz tub of sour cream

1 teaspoon Montreal seasoning

½ orange

1. Mix the cucumber, celery, onion, Montreal seasoning, and juice from the orange with the sour cream.
2. Set in the refrigerator while preparing the fish.
3. Mix the vinegar, soy sauce, olive oil, tarragon seasoning, sage, lemon pepper, and juice from 1 lemon.
4. In a glass dish, place the steaks in the marinade.
5. Marinate for ½ hour, then turn the fish over and marinate for another 30 minutes.
6. Place the swordfish steaks on a medium hot grill.
7. Grill about 3-5 minutes per side or until the meat is white and flaky.
8. Serve with cucumber sauce.
9. Enjoy during the Marlins game.

Grilled Swordfish

Key Lime Pie

15 egg yolks

1-14 ounce can sweetened condensed milk

½ cup key lime or lime juice

1 graham cracker pie shell

1. Beat the egg yolks.
2. Add the condensed milk.
3. Add the lime juice.
4. Stir well.
5. Pour the mixture in the pie shell.
6. Bake in the oven for 15 minutes at 350 degrees.
7. Chill in the refrigerator for at least 1 hour.
8. Enjoy during the Marlins game.

Key Lime Pie

Bratwurst

8 bratwurst	Mustard
3 bottles beer	Sauerkraut
Buns	Any other condiments you may like

1. Pour 3 bottles of beer in a large cooking pan.
2. Heat the beer so it is hot.
3. Put the bratwursts in the hot beer.
4. Cover with a lid and let the brats simmer in the beer for 20 minutes.
5. Now transfer the brats to the barbeque grill.
6. Grill for several minutes on each side.
7. Steam the buns, or microwave them for 30 seconds.
8. Place a brat in a bun with sauerkraut and mustard.
9. Enjoy during the Brewers game.

Bratwurst

Cheddar Cheese Soup

4 tablespoons butter

1 small chopped onion

½ teaspoon garlic powder

½ cup white flour

2 cups chicken stock

2 cups milk

1 cup heavy cream

5 cups grated cheddar cheese

½ teaspoon cayenne pepper

6 slices crisp bacon, crumbled

½ cup chopped celery

½ cup sliced carrots

½ cup chopped potatoes

1. Fry the bacon, set aside and crumble when cool.

2. Melt the butter and saute' the onion , celery, carrots, and potato in a skillet until the onion is translucent.

3. Whisk the flour in the chicken stock and mix with the milk and cream.

4. In a soup pan, mix the bacon, vegetables, and liquid. Cook on low heat.

5. Add the garlic and pepper.

6. While stirring, add in the cheese.

7. Continue stirring until the cheese is melted. Do not boil.

8. Sprinkle cheese on top and serve during the Brewers game.

Cheddar Cheese Soup

Crunch Fried Walleye

8-Walleye fillets (or other fish)

2 cups corn flakes

2 cups cheddar cheese crackers

1 cup panko crumbs

½ cup grated parmesan cheese

1 teaspoon ground black pepper

½ teaspoon oregano

½ teaspoon grated ginger root

3 eggs

¼ cup milk

Vegetable oil

Tartar sauce

1 cup mayonaisse

½ diced onion

2 tablespoons pickle relish

2 tablespoons mustard

1 teaspoon lemon zest

Juice from 1 lemon

½ teaspoon grated ginger root

½ teaspoon ground black pepper

1 teaspoon dill seasoning

1. Mix all the ingredients for tartar sauce in a bowl and refrigerate while cooking the fish.

2. Blend milk and eggs in a separate dish.

3. In a food processor blend the corn flakes, crackers, crumbs, parmesan cheese, pepper, oregano, and ginger root. The consistency should be like crumbs.

4. Dip each fillet in the egg milk blend and coat each filet with the crumb mixture. Place each filet in a frying pan with very hot vegetable oil.

5. Cook each side until golden brown or until fish is flaky. Serve with tartar sauce during the Twins game.

Crunch Fried Walleye

Blueberry Muffins

1 ½ cups flour

½ cup sugar

2 teaspoons baking powder

1 teaspoon baking soda

1/3 cup vegetable oil

1 egg

1/3 cup milk

3 cups fresh blueberries

Butter flavored cooking oil spray

Butter

Muffin pan

1. Mix the dry ingredients in a bowl.
2. In another bowl mix the oil, egg, and milk.
3. Mix the 2 bowls of ingredients together.
4. Gently fold in the blueberries.
5. Spray the muffin pan with the oil spray.
6. Spoon the mixture into a muffin tin so each muffin is level to the top of the pan.
7. Bake in a 400 degree oven for 20-25 minutes or until done.
8. Spread butter inside the hot muffins and enjoy during the Twins game.

Blueberry Muffins

New York Steak

2 New York Steaks
1 lime
1 teaspoon garlic powder

1 teaspoon parsley
Ground salt
Ground pepper

New York Steak

1. Squeeze lime juice on both sides of the steaks.
2. Sprinkle garlic powder on both sides of the steaks.
3. Crush the salt and pepper in a dish.
4. Rub the salt and pepper on both sides of the steaks.
5. Use salt and pepper to taste.
6. On high heat, sear both sides of the steaks for about 2 minutes per side.
7. Reduce heat to medium and grill to your liking.
8. Enjoy during the Mets game.

Lox and Bagels

6-8 of your favorite bagels   1 cucumber, sliced

1 package cream cheese   1 lemon

1 small jar capers   1 package smoked salmon

1 tomato, sliced   Salt

1 onion, sliced or chopped   Pepper

1. Toast the bagels.
2. Spread the cream cheese on each bagel.
3. Place capers in the cream cheese.
4. Layer sliced or chopped onion with slices of the salmon a sliced tomato on each bagel.
5. Squeeze a little lemon juice over the tomato.
6. Salt and pepper to taste.
7. Enjoy during the Mets game.

Lox and Bagels

New York Pizza

Dough

1 teaspoon active dry yeast

¾ cup warm water

2-3 cups flour

1 teaspoon salt

1 tablespoon vegetable oil

1 teaspoon sugar

Sauce

1-12 ounce can tomato sauce

1 pound shredded mozzarella cheese

1-8 ounce package cream cheese

¾ cup Romano cheese

1 teaspoon dried oregano

12-15 slices pepperoni

6-8 mushrooms sliced

Other toppings as desired

1. In a bowl dissolve yeast, salt and sugar in warm water.
2. In another bowl, add vegetable oil and 2 cups flour and stir. Add extra flour if needed
3. Add yeast to dough and knead for a few minutes.
4. Roll dough into a ball and put in a bowl with a little vegetable oil spread over the top. Cover.
5. Let rise for 2 or 3 hours, then put the dough in the refrigerator overnight.
6. Next day, hand toss the dough or roll the dough out to about a 12 inch circle.
7. Cover the dough with tomato sauce sprinkle oregano and add Mozzarella cheese.
8. Spread small chunks of cream cheese and Romano cheese over the pizza.
9. If desired, spread pepperoni and mushrooms evenly on the pizza.
10. Place the pizza on a hot pizza stone in the oven.
11. Cook for 12-15 minutes at 500 degrees.
12. Enjoy during the Yankees game.

New York Pizza

Knish

8 medium potatoes

½ cube butter

½ cup minced onion

4 tablespoons chicken broth

Salt to taste

Pepper to taste

2 small red peppers, chopped

6 sheets phyllo dough

1. Boil potatoes until tender.
2. In a large bowl, mash potatoes
3. Saute' onions and pepper in 1/2 the butter.
4. Mix onions, peppers, potatoes, broth, salt, and pepper.
5. Lay out 3 sheets of phyllo dough and cut in half. Repeat.
6. Spoon mixture on 1 section of phyllo dough.
7. Put another section on top of mixture.
8. Repeat with other sections of dough.
9. Melt butter and brush over each one.
10. Bake at 375 degrees for 35 minutes or until golden brown.
11. Makes 12.
12. Eat during the Yankee game.

Knish

Shrimp Tostada

1 pound cooked shrimp

1-15 ounce can black beans

1-15 ounce can diced tomatoes and green chilies (spicy)

½ cup chopped cilantro

1 diced medium onion

Tostada shells

Shredded lettuce

Shredded cabbage

2 diced avocados

Shredded cheese

Vegetable oil

1 lime

1 teaspoon salt

1. Saute' the shrimp in hot vegetable oil. Then remove the tails.
2. Drain the tomato and chilies and mix with the cilantro, onion, avocado and salt. Squeeze lime juice in the mixture.
3. Stir in the shrimp.
4. Drain the black beans and spread a spoonful over a tostada.
5. Sprinkle a handful of cheese over the beans.
6. Heat in a microwave for 30 seconds.
7. Spoon a generous portion of the shrimp mix over the tostada.
8. Add some lettuce and cabbage over the top.
9. Enjoy during the A's game.

Shrimp Tostada

Won Tons

1 package large won ton squares

2 pounds ground beef

1-14 ounce can Chinese mixed vegetables

2-10 ounce cans mushroom soup

1-8 ounce can water chestnuts

1 teaspoon celery salt

1 teaspoon ground black pepper

2 tablespoons soy sauce

1 teaspoon beef bullion

1 beaten egg

Vegetable oil

1. Cook ground beef in a pan, then drain.
2. Stir in mixed vegetables, soup, water chestnuts, celery salt, soy sauce, pepper, and bullion.
3. Heat for 2 minutes.
4. Spoon 2 or 3 tablespoons of mixture on 1 large won ton wrap.
5. Wrap won ton over the beef mix and seal edges by brushing on a small amount of egg.
6. Place filled won tons in a pan with hot vegetable oil.
7. Cook each side until golden brown.
8. Dip in soy sauce.
9. Eat during the Athletics game.

Won Tons

Philly Cheesesteak

1 diced red bell pepper

1 diced green bell pepper

1 chopped large onion

2 pounds thinly sliced beef

1 pound thinly sliced provolone cheese

1 teaspoon Italian seasoning

Salt

Pepper

Garlic powder

Vegetable oil

Butter

Italian rolls, sliced lengthwise

1. In hot vegetable oil and butter, cook onion until translucent.
2. Add in peppers and continue cooking and stirring over high heat until peppers are soft.
3. Season to taste with garlic, salt, and pepper.
4. Turn heat down and layer with beef.
5. When hot, layer with cheese.
6. Sprinkle Italian seasoning over the cheese.
7. Cover pan until cheese is melted.
8. With a spatula, put a generous amount of mixture in an Italian roll.
9. Enjoy during the Phillies game.

Philly Cheesesteak

Philly Sticky Buns

This recipe has 3 parts

The Dough
1/3 cup milk

¼ cup sugar

½ teaspoon salt

½ cube butter

¼ cup warm water

1 package active dry yeast

1 egg

2-3 cups flour

The Filling
½ cube butter

½ cup brown sugar

½ cup raisins

½ teaspoon cinnamon

½ teaspoon nutmeg

½ cup walnuts or pecans or mixed nuts

Bottom of Pan
½ cube butter

¼ cup brown sugar

½ teaspoon cinnamon

½ teaspoon nutmeg

Philly Sticky Buns

1. Mix sugar, yeast, salt and flour.
2. Add warm water, warm milk and soft butter and mix for 3 minutes.
3. Add egg and more flour if needed and continue mixing.
4. Let dough rise for 2 hours.
5. Mix all the filling ingredients.
6. Mix all the pan ingredients
7. Spread pan ingredients in bottom of pan or casserole dish.
8. After dough has risen roll it out flat.
9. Spread the filling on the dough and roll it up.
10. Cut buns 3 -5 inches apart and place in the pan over the pan ingredients.
11. Cook in oven at 350 degrees for 20 minutes.
12. Eat during the Phillies game.

Chipped Ham Sandwich

1 pound very thinly sliced ham luncheon meat

Hamburger style buns

Favorite barbeque sauce

1. In a large cooking pan heat up the ham slices.
2. Toast or steam the buns.
3. On low heat, stir in your favorite barbeque sauce.
4. When heated through, spoon a generous portion on the bun.
5. Enjoy during the Pirate game.

Chipped Ham Sandwich

Pittsburgh Salad

1- 12 oz. package lettuce and greens

1 small sliced cucumber

1 small diced red onion

1 sliced avacodo

1 tomato cut in wedges

Sliced mushrooms

1 grilled chicken breast sliced

2 cups shredded cheese

Lots of french fries

Any salad dressing

1. Grill the chicken breast, slice and set aside.
2. In a large bowl add lettuce and greens.
3. Stir in the cucumber, onion and mushrooms.
4. Decorate the top with tomato and avacado.
5. Layer the top with the chicken slices.
6. Put a big bunch of cooked french fries on top.
7. Sprinkle the cheese over the top.
8. Serve in salad dishes with your favorite dressing
9. Enjoy during the Pirate game.

Pittsburgh Salad

St. Louis Pizza

2-14 ounce cans tomatoes

12 ounce can tomato paste

2 tablespoons dark corn syrup

1½ teaspoons salt

1 teaspoon dry basil

1 teaspoon dry oregano

1 teaspoon dry thyme

2 cups cheddar cheese

2 cups swiss cheese

2 cups provolone cheese

1 tablespoon hickory liquid smoke

4 cups flour

1 teaspoon salt

1 tablespoon baking powder

1 tablespoon cornstarch

1 cup water

1. Shred all the cheese and mix together, add liquid smoke to the cheese and mix. If desired vary the amount of each cheese. Set aside.

2. In a separate bowl pour in the cans of tomatoes, cutting them up. Mix in the tomato paste.

3. Add 1 tablespoon of corn syrup.

4. Add in ½ teaspoon salt, basil, oregano, and thyme. Set aside.

5. In a separate bowl mix the flour, 1 teaspoon salt, baking powder, and cornstarch.

6. Add 1 cup water and mix together to form a dough, adding a extra flour if needed. Keep the dough stiff and dry.

7. Divide the dough into 4 balls, roll out each ball of dough and hand toss.

8. Roll into thin 10-12 inch diameter.

9. Add tomato sauce to the pizza and add cheese to the pizza.

10. Heat a pizza stone for each pizza at 450 degrees for 15 minutes in an oven.

11. Cook each pizza for 12-15 minutes at 450 degrees in an oven.

12. Enjoy during the Cardinals game.

St. Louis Pizza

Toasted Ravioli

Vegetable oil for frying

1 cup buttermilk

1 cup Italian bread crumbs

1 cup cornmeal or instant Polenta Mix

12 oz. ravioli

¼ cup grated parmesan cheese

Marinara Sauce

1. Heat the oil.
2. Mix bread crumbs and Polenta in a bowl.
3. Pour buttermilk in a separate bowl.
4. Dip the ravioli in buttermilk, then into crumb mixture.
5. Fry the ravioli in oil turning occasionally for about 3 minutes until brown.
6. Sprinkle with parmesan and serve with marinara sauce.

Toasted Ravioli

Fish Tacos

8-10 white fish filets (cod, tilapia, mahi mahi, pollock)

Peanut oil

1 egg

2 cups flour

¼ cup parmesan cheese

2 tablespoons cornstarch

1 teaspoon baking powder

1 small bottle beer

1 teaspoon salt

Shredded cabbage

Corn tortillas

Salsa

Hot sauce

1. In a frying pan heat the oil medium hot.
2. Put I cup flour in a separate bowl.
3. In another bowl mix the rest of the flour, parmesan cheese, cornstarch, baking powder, and salt.
4. Stir in the egg and beer and make a good batter.
5. In the first bowl, coat each fish with flour.
6. Dip each fish filet in the batter.
7. Cook each filet in the hot oil about 3-5 minutes per side.
8. Set aside to drain.
9. Fry each tortilla in the hot oil about 30 seconds per side.
10. Set aside to cool for a few minutes.
11. Place fish in each tortilla.
12. Add cabbage, salsa, and or hot sauce to each tortilla.
13. Enjoy during the Padres game.

Fish Tacos

Taquitos

3 chicken breasts, cooked and shredded.

2 Anaheim peppers, diced

1 bunch cilantro, chopped

1 onion, diced

16 ounces whipped cream cheese

30 corn tortillas

2 tablespoons chipotle seasoning

Vegetable oil

Salsa

Guacamole

1. Mix peppers, cilantro, onion, and chipotle with the cream cheese.
2. Put wet paper towels over and under tortillas in a microwave for about 30 seconds. (This makes them easier to roll up without breaking.)
3. Put 2 tablespoons of cream cheese filling in each tortilla.
4. Add a layer of shredded chicken in each tortilla.
5. Put a toothpick in each tortilla to hold it together.
6. Deep fry in vegetable oil until golden brown.
7. Dip in salsa or guacamole.
8. Enjoy during the Padres game.

Taquitos

Dungeness Crab

1 or more Dungeness crabs (live or whole cooked). If crab is pre-cooked make sure the legs curl underneath and do not hang.

½ cup or more salt

3 or 4 lemon wedges

½ stick melted butter

1. In a large cooking pan place the live or previously cooked crab in salted boiling water. (1/2 cup salt per gallon of water).
2. If crab is live boil for 15-18 minutes.
3. If crab is pre-cooked boil until meat is hot, maybe 1 or 2 minutes.
4. Take crab out of boiling water and let it cool or run water on it to cool it for cleaning.
5. Pull away the back shell from the crab. Turn the crab over and pull the triangular section away.
6. Turn the crab again and scrape away the gills and intestines.
7. Wash the crab clean.
8. Twist off the legs.
9. Break the crab in half and continue rinsing.
10. With a mallet or back of a knife, crack the legs.
11. Use a fork to dig out the crab meat.
12. Squeeze lemon juice over the meat.
13. Dip in melted butter and enjoy the wonderful crab flavor during the Giants game.

Dungeness Crab

Chocolate Cake with Ghirardelli Squares

1 ½ cups flour

1 cup shredded baking chocolate

1 cup sugar

1 ½ teaspoons baking soda

½ teaspoon salt

2/3 cup shortening

1 cup buttermilk

3 small eggs

1 ½ teaspoon vanilla

10-15 Ghirardelli chocolate squares with caramel.

frosting

1-8 ounce package cream cheese softened

½ stick butter, softened

1 teaspoon vanilla

1 tablespoon milk

3 cups powdered sugar

2 tablespoons cocoa

Ghirardelli chocolate squares (any flavor)

1. Mix flour, chocolate, sugar, baking soda, and salt together.
2. On low speed in a mixer add in shortening, buttermilk, eggs, and vanilla.
3. Pour batter in 2-8 inch round pans, greased.
4. Put caramel chocolate squares throughout the batter.
5. Bake at 350 degrees for 30-35 minutes.
6. After cooling, put cakes on 2 plates and frost.
7. Put both layers together.

frosting

Chocolate Cake with Ghirardelli Squares

1. Mix cream cheese, butter, and vanilla together.
2. Stir in milk, powdered sugar, and cocoa, until smooth.
3. Add in a little more milk if needed (1 tablespoon at a time).
4. Layer the frosted cake with any flavor of Ghirardelli chocolate squares.
5. Eat during the last inning of the Giant game.

Grilled Salmon

4 Salmon filets or steaks   2/3 cup brown sugar

1 cup soy sauce   Juice from 2 limes

1 cup apple vinegar   Montreal seasoning

½ cup canola or olive oil

1. Score the salmon and lightly sprinkle with Montreal seasoning on both sides.
2. Let fish sit in refrigerator for 1 hour.
3. In a large bowl mix the soy sauce, vinegar, olive oil, brown sugar, and lime juice.
4. Remove the salmon from the refrigerator and place in the bowl with the liquid mixture.
5. Marinate in the refrigerator for 2-3 hours.
6. Sear both sides of the salmon on high heat.
7. Continue grilling on medium heat for about 5-7 minutes per side.
8. Do not overcook. If it is slightly rare in the center it is good to eat.
9. Enjoy during the Mariners game.

Grilled Salmon

Fish Chowder

1 small onion chopped

2 carrots sliced

2 stalks celery chopped

1 large potato diced

4 slices bacon chopped

1-15 oz. can chicken broth

1-15 oz. can corn

1 pound haddock or other white fish

1-7 oz. can clams

2 cups half and half

4 tablespoons flour

2 teaspoons curry

¼ teaspoon black pepper

Salt to taste

Fish Chowder

1. Cook the bacon bits until crisp. Set the bacon aside.
2. Saute onions, carrots, and celery in the bacon fat until onions are translucent.
3. Mix the flour with the half and half until it is smooth. Pour into a large soup pan with the chicken broth.
4. Add the potatoes and cook on low heat for 30 minutes.
5. Add the fish, corn, clams and juice, curry, onions, carrots, celery, and black pepper and cook for 20-30 more minutes.
6. Enjoy during the Mariners game.

Mango Fish

8 tilapia, sole, mahi mahi, or whitefish filets

1 cup olive oil

1 minced garlic clove

1 teaspoon dried basil

1 teaspoon curry powder

1 tablespoon ground black pepper

1 teaspoon salt

2 teaspoons grated ginger root

1 tablespoon brown sugar

Salsa

2 chopped mangos

2 chopped nectarines

Juice from ½ orange

Juice from ½ lemon

1 teaspoon orange zest

1 teaspoon lemon zest

½ chopped red onion

1 chopped jalapeno pepper

1 chopped red bell pepper

2 tablespoons cilantro

1 teaspoon ground black pepper

1 teaspoon brown sugar

1 chopped avacodo

1. In a dish mix the olive oil, garlic, basil, curry, pepper, salt, ginger, and brown sugar together.

2. Marinate the fish filets in mixture for 1-2 hours in the refrigerator.

3. Make the salsa.

4. In a dish, add the mangos, nectarines, orange juice, lemon juice, orange zest, lemon zest, onion, jalapeno, bell pepper, cilantro, black pepper, brown sugar and mix together.

5. Do not add the avocado at this time.

6. Marinate in the refrigerator for 1-2 hours.

Mango Fish

7. After marinating, place the filets in an oven pan.

8. Spoon about 1-2 teaspoons of salsa on each filet.

9. Save most of the salsa for later.

10. Bake in the oven at 375 degrees for 12 minutes or until the fish flakes off easily.

11. Add the avocado to the remainder of the salsa and spoon about 1 tablespoon of salsa on to each filet.

12. Enjoy during the Rays game.

Coconut Shrimp

20 or 30 jumbo shrimp-deveined

2 cups Panko crumbs

2 cups unsweetened or sweetened coconut flakes

3 beaten eggs

Vegetable oil

1. Dip the shrimp in the egg to coat.
2. Mix the Panko crumbs and coconut together.
3. Roll the shrimp in the crumb coconut mixture.
4. Cook in hot oil in a frying pan or deep fryer on medium heat.
5. Fry for 2 to 4 minutes or until done.
6. Serve during the Rays game.

Coconut Shrimp

Texas Barbecue Brisket

Beef brisket (3 lbs.-15 lbs)

I used 3 pounds for a small party

Montreal Seasoning

Barbecue sauce

1 cup tomato paste

1 cup brown sugar

1 cup apple cider vinegar

1 teaspoon ground red pepper

1 teaspoon ground garlic

½ teaspoon salt

½ teaspoon ground black pepper

½ teaspoon sage

½ teaspoon celery salt

1. 24 hours before cooking, rub Montreal seasoning all over the brisket.
2. Cover and refrigerate.
3. Cook in covered grill for 3 hours at 200 degrees.
4. Take off grill and slice the brisket.
5. Cover with Bar B Q sauce in a pan.
6. Put back on the grill for another hour.
7. Barbecue sauce
8. Mix tomato paste, brown sugar, and vinegar in a bowl.
9. Add seasonings.
10. Add more tomato paste, brown sugar, or apple cider vinegar according to taste.
11. Enjoy during the Ranger game.

Texas Barbecue Brisket

Texas Chili

1 pound bacon fried and broken up into 1-2 inch pieces

2 pounds ground beef

2 pounds beef stew bits

1-15 ounce can pinto beans

1-15 ounce black beans

1 diced pasilla pepper

1 diced anaheim pepper

1 diced bell pepper

3 diced serrano peppers

1 diced onion

¾ cup molasses

1-15 ounce can tomato sauce

6-7 diced tomatoes

3 cloves crushed garlic

½ cup minced cilantro

½ cup minced parsley

3 tablespoons cumin

1 tablespoon oregano

1 tablespoon cayenne pepper

1 tablespoon chili powder

Salt

Pepper

Shredded cheddar cheese

Sour cream

1 cup water

1. Fry bacon, break up and set aside

2. Saute peppers and onions, then put in a stock pot.

3. Fry stew bits in the bacon grease, then add to the stock pot.

4. Fry the ground beef and add to the pot.

5. Turn the pot on low to medium heat and stir.

6. Add the bacon to the pot.

7. Add tomatoes, molasses, tomato sauce, and garlic and stir.

8. Add beans and stir.

9. Add in the cilantro, parsley, cumin, oregano, cayenne pepper and chili powder. Stir.

10. Add salt and pepper to taste.

11. Let cook on very low heat for an hour to marinate all the flavors.

12. Put shredded cheese and sour cream on top of each bowl of chili as desired.

13. Enjoy during the Rangers game.

Texas Chili

Street Meat Dogs

All beef hot dogs

1 diced onion

2-3 diced hot peppers

1 chopped tomato

1 chopped cucumber

Mustard

Corn relish

Yellow hot dog buns

1. Score the hot dogs, then put them in very hot water and simmer for 20 minutes.
2. Steam the buns.
3. Put the dogs in the buns and add onions, peppers, tomatoes, and cucumber.
4. Squeeze on some mustard.
5. Garnish with a lot of corn relish.
6. Enjoy during the Blue Jay game.

Street Meat Dogs

French Toast

4 eggs

Several slices french bread or other bread

½ cup cream

Maple syrup

Butter

Whipped cream or topping

Sliced strawberries or blueberries

1. Beat the eggs.
2. Stir in the cream, cinnamon, nutmeg, and vanilla.
3. Melt some butter on a griddle pan for coating.
4. Dip the bread in the egg mixture.
5. Fry on both sides on the melted butter.
6. When cooked all the way through put the slices on individual plates.
7. Spread butter on each toast.
8. Add syrup, whipped cream and fruit.
9. Enjoy during the Blue Jays game.

French Toast

Virginia Ham

5-10 pound ham	1 cup brown sugar
1 mango	¼ cup molasses
1 small onion	1 tablespoon orange zest
1 red chili pepper	2 fresh oranges (squeeze the juice)
1 green bell pepper	1 Tablespoon dijon mustard
2-3 inches fresh ginger root, peeled	1 can pinapple rings with juice

1. In a food processor, blend the mango, onion, peppers, and ginger.
2. Add in the brown sugar, molasses, orange zest, orange juice, pineapple juice, and mustard.
3. Place the ham in a baking pan.
4. Pour mixture over the ham.
5. Bake in oven at 350 degrees for 2-3 hours or until a meat thermometer reads 160 degrees.
6. Eat during the Nationals game.

Virginia Ham

Cherry Cream Pie

4 envelopes dream whip

3 cups milk

1 cup cream

2-8 ounce packages cream cheese

2-21 ounce cans cherry pie filling

2 graham cracker pie crusts

2 ounce package vanilla jello

1. Put milk and cream in a large dish.
2. Add dream whip, cream cheese, and vanilla jello and beat with an electric mixer until it thickens.
3. Pour mixture in the pie crusts.
4. Refrigerate for 1 hour.
5. Pour the cherry filling over the cream mix.
6. Enjoy during the Nationals game.

Cherry Cream Pie

Index of Recipes

54544832R00038

Made in the USA
Columbia, SC
02 April 2019